Selah, are  whisper? V .... ~~the~~ Book of Psalms as a reminder for us to ponder or a musical pause for us to remember? Is your presence an exclamation point or a place for our soul to linger? I believe you are a reminder to take time for the Holy Spirit to inspire.

After each verse where *Selah* appears, *The Amplified Bible* (AMPC) reads, "pause and calmly think about that." So when we see the word *Selah* in the Psalms or elsewhere, as in Habakkuk 3, it is a signal for us to pause and carefully weigh the meaning of what we have just read or heard, lifting up our hearts in praise to God for His great truths.

Psalm 66:4 (AMPC)
"All the earth shall bow down to You; and sing [praises] to You; they shall praise Your name in song. Selah [pause, and calmly think of that]!"

Raw,

Barely Edited,

Heart-Driven,

Heavenly-Given,

Prayerful Musings

Musing ~

A meditation, contemplation, deliberation, pondering,
reflection, introspection,
deep calling unto deep.

When you muse long enough in company with
the Creator, you can begin to experience a quickening
heartbeat in His presence,
making you passionate about His purposes
and prayerful regarding His promises.

Introduction

Inside are my personal journaling thoughts. For many years, my habit has been to pick up a journal and write when thoughts and images came to mind. At times it was after I sat quietly in prayer or worship. I didn't try to edit them. I wanted to leave them in their original state. I assumed that if I didn't write as a professional writer or poet, they would be for my eyes only. Now, however, I have decided that printing them becomes my personal legacy writing to share with anyone who desires to read and hear how one heart, mine in particular, thinks about life and her relationship with Father God, Lord Jesus, and the Holy Spirit.

Poetry

Poetry on pages
Life in rhythm
Symmetry by sages.
Who has set the meter?
Who ordered the lane?
Where can its author be found?
Is it joy or pain?

I read somewhere that David Carradine said, "If you can't be a poet, be the poem." The Bible in Ephesians 2:10 reads, *"For we are God's workmanship, created in Christ Jesus to do good works, which God prepared in advance for us to do."* The Greek word for workmanship is *poiema,* which is where English speakers get the word *poem.* It can also be defined as a creative masterpiece.

You, dear reader, are God's poetic,
creative masterpiece.

Surprise

I threw myself in reckless abandon on God,
And to my delighted surprise,
It was a sure-footed thrust.

Proverbs 3:26

"For the Lord will be your confidence
and will keep your foot from being snared."

Run!

The lion roars
the trumpet blasts
who could but run!

The mission set
the calling sure
who could but go!

The Voice of the Trumpet when heard
is a compelling force to obey the Word.

1 Corinthians 9:24 and 26a (AMPC)

"Do you not know that in a race all the runners compete, but [only] one receives the prize? So run [your race] that you may lay hold [of the prize] and make it yours."

"Therefore I do not run uncertainly
(without definite aim).

Breathing with and in Him

Yes, Lord, make me a revelation. I long to be a revelation
of Your goodness, breathing out favor and inhaling faith,
a living epistle of Jesus my Lord.
I pant to be to the praise of Your glory
as I become Your revealed story.

Psalm 119:131 (AMPC)

*"I opened my mouth and panted
[with eager desire], for I longed for
Your commandments."*

Words

The mind, a womb, receives life's seed from the heart
and is impregnated by our spoken declaration.
Let our words be full of life.

Proverbs 15:4 (AMPC)

*"A gentle tongue [with its healing power] is a tree of life,
but willful contrariness in it breaks down the spirit."*

Psalm 71:18 (AMPC)

*"Yes, even when I am old and gray-headed, O God,
forsake me not, [but keep me alive] until I have declared
Your mighty strength to {this} generation, and
Your might and power to all that are to come."*

In Between

What person can say who holds each day?
One thing is for sure, His love is secure.
In fullness of time, all will be seen.
Only for a short while are we caught in between.
Until the day He calls us home,
we will gladly worship our Father
and make Him well-known.

John 14: 2,3

"In my Father's house are many rooms; if it were not
so, I would have told you. I am going there to
prepare a place for you. And if I go and prepare a
place for you, I will come back and take you to be with
me that you also may be where I am. You know the
way to the place where I am going."

Friend of Like Mind

My heart is enlarged
a place well-made.
The foundation of Jesus
is fully laid.
I cannot withstand any more delay
for the canter of my Lord
is pounding away.
My Father is speaking...

Heart, be still,
too wildly you're leaping.
My heart's passion is His call.
My temple is His command.

Friend of like mind, take my hand.
Let us find in each the common goal;
a willingness to put our lives on the altar
and a plea,
"Send me, Lord, I'll go!"

Isaiah 6:8

"Then I heard the voice of the Lord saying, 'Whom shall I send? And who will go for us?' And I said, 'Here am I. Send me!'"

Matthew 28:19

"Therefore go and make disciples of all nations, baptizing them in the name of the Father and of the Son and of the Holy Spirit, and teaching them to obey everything I have commanded you. And surely I am with you always, to the very end of the age."

Step Out

As you step out as an ambassador of the light of His transforming Good News, you will encounter souls driven into dark and hidden caves. Some will stand at the entrance, looking both ways: light, darkness, light, darkness. Which pull is stronger? Others may try to recede even farther from the light into the deep darkness that blinds their soul.

As you approach, you are His light bearer. The Light of the world, Jesus Christ, your Lord and Savior, will expel the darkness! Keep praying. Remember love, mercy, and grace can prevail. Weren't you drawn like a moth to a flame?

Have faith. Release love. Proclaim.

Matthew 5:14

*"You are the light of the world.
A city built on a hill cannot be hidden."*

John 8:12

*"When Jesus spoke again to the people,
he said, "I am the light of the world. Whoever follows me
will never walk in darkness, but will have the light of life."*

John the Baptist

John, the shadow sent before the form,
preparing the way for us to be reborn.
John clothed himself in camel's hair,
the garment of rebellion that brings a snare.
Jesus put on our sin so we may put on Him.
Hear the voice of one in the wilderness,
eating locusts and honey for his sustenance.
Oh yes, the voice can still be heard.
It's the amplified voice of the Word!
Turn, repent, and choose what you shall eat:
the locusts of wrath or the honey of redemption.
Who shall you be?
"Live," compels God Almighty. "Choose Me."
Become vocal chords of praise.
Rise higher! Cause heads to lift and eyes to raise.
Surely goodness and mercy
will follow you all your days.

Isaiah 57:14

"And it will be said: 'Build up, build up, prepare the road! Remove the obstacles out of the way of my people.'"

Luke 7:27

"This is the one about whom it is written: 'I will send my messenger ahead of you, who will prepare your way before you.'"

Honor

Can you not see the privilege and honor King Jesus has set before you? Must there be crowns and visible glory? Or are you willing to see as Heavenly Father sees the value of His creation within a life?

Some see only cravings for more. They ache without hope. Some see impossibilities, worthless efforts, and hard work.

What do you see when you look at humanity? What would you consider His highest honor?

Each vessel is precious; for each life Jesus died.

Consider

Consider your ways
Be restored and surrender
Open your heart
Stay willing and tender
Put things in order
Observe and then do
Consider the Lord
And His love for you
Seek an eternal gain
To profit your way
Know God is willing
Listen and obey
Give of Love's first measure
Then receive heaven's return
Storing up eternal treasure
Following after His concern

2 Corinthians 4:7

"But we have this treasure in jars of clay to show
this all-surpassing power is from
God and not from us."
Could there be a greater privilege than being Father's
oracle to His creation, to humankind?

Psalm 89: 15

"Blessed are those who have learned
to acclaim you, who walk in the light of your presence,
LORD."

Revelation 4:11 (AMPC)

"You are worthy, our Lord and God, to receive glory and
honor and power, for you created all things, and by your
will they were created and have their being."

The Kingdom of God

It's more than a what. It's a Who.
It's His presence — His power. It's you.
It's Him and His rule and reign.
It's His goodness, His glory — your gain.
It's hope, the way, and reward.
It's Jesus Christ where and when
He is LORD.

Mercy's Lead

Mercy, impetus to zeal,
compassion, forerunner of the purging,
fiery consummation of His justice,
overtake my soul!

Mercy, you are the catalyst
that thrusts me fervently forward.
You cry out, "Seek Him. Seek His righteousness. Seek
His Kingdom."

Mercy's obtaining price shall ever remain the same.
"Give me away," she cries. "Proclaim Jesus' holy name."
When you thrust through mercy's side
No violation can abide.
From her fountain flows love's release.
In her bounty all sin does cease.

Hear the lion roar — His name is Jesus.
See the stripes He bore — His name is Jesus.

"If you love me less, shall I not love you more?"
Shall I do despite the spirit of grace
and the stripes Jesus bore?
Mercy honors grace
and pays the tribute that is due.
Heart, be enlarged toward your sister and brother.
Please the One who is faithful and true.

1 Peter 1:3, 4, 5

"Praise be to the God and Father of our Lord Jesus
Christ! In his great mercy, he has given us new birth into a
living hope through the resurrection of Jesus Christ from
the dead, and into an inheritance that can never perish,
spoil or fade-kept in heaven for you, who through faith are
shielded by God's power until the coming of the salvation
that is ready to be revealed in the last time."

Hope's Anchor

Be prepared with your declaration of hope
Discipled by faith and meekness.
The testimony of God's goodness
Will no longer be delivered in weakness.
The dowry of God's love is our gospel story.
Our inheritance of hope begins now
As joint heirs of His glory.

Power

You've called them out,
Lord, from the regions of the damned.
The borders of hell, fear, and doubt have fallen,
and they are released.
Be still, my soul.
Know that He alone is God,
and watch as He sets the captives free.

Isaiah 49:9

"...say to the captives, 'Come out,'
and to those in darkness,
'Be free!'"

Psalm 46:10

"Be still, and know that I am God;
I will be exalted among the nations,
I will be exalted in the earth."

Zechariah 2:13

"Be still before the LORD, all mankind,
because he has roused himself from
his holy dwelling."

God to God Again

We, the statement of God's enduring mercy,
are endeavoring to know His Word
and follow His ways.
Ah yes, not only to be in the heart of God,
a part of His very self,
but to operate in His ways.
And why would that be?
So we can become the heartbeat
and outraying of His deity.

Then we, the collective blending of His voice,
become the full circle,
as a rainbow when seen from the air
is from God to God again.

Revelation 15:3b

"Great and marvelous are your deeds,
Lord God Almighty.
Just and true are your ways, King of the ages."

He Is Jesus

Intimate moments one by one
Build a life-long bond with the Holy One.
His tender heart's waiting
To reveal His loving Son.
And to whom shall He make known His will?
To each panting soul that longs to be won.
This is life.
This is beauty.
He is Jesus
Not just duty.
Not dry or boring
But sweet and knowing.
Oh, how His presence sparkles.
My heart beholds and marvels.
This is life
This is beauty.
He is Jesus
Not just duty
He will lift, compel, and draw until
we're enveloped in reverent awe!

Isaiah 61:3

"... provide for those who grieve in Zion — to bestow on them a crown of beauty instead of ashes, the oil of joy instead of mourning, and a garment of praise instead of a spirit of despair. They will be called oaks of righteousness, a planting of the LORD for the display of his splendor."

Loss and Gain

While we were yet sinners, the Bible exclaims,
While we were yet sinners, our value remains!
On the cross, His loss was our loss;
By His resurrection, His gain is our gain!

John 11:25

"Jesus said to her,
'I am the resurrection and the life.
The one who believes in me will live,
even though he dies; and whoever lives and
believes in me will never die.'"

Be

To be like Him, our God, the Creator;
To be a life-giver and vessel of creation
in another person's life;
To be allowed an impact in what
He has already fashioned;
To craft with the Master Craftsman;
To touch and be of value to
His anointed with a helping hand.

To esteem highly that which
He has conferred worthy of all honor—
His creation, all Jesus died to redeem.
I have found myself within my Love's voice.
I have become a sound pattern of His presence.

Psalms 29:4

"The voice of the LORD is powerful;
the voice of the LORD is majestic."

Reality Is Thee

Glimpses of faith
Glimpses of charity
Glimpses of hope's abiding clarity
Visions of glory
Visions of grace
Visions of a well-run race
Forever forgiven
Forever free
Forever covenanted with Thee.
Newness of walk
Newness of peace
Newness of living — what a release
Reality of Christ arisen in me
Reality, His strength - Reality, His power
Reality is Thee, Lord, every hour.

Colossians 2:17

"These are a shadow of the things that were to come; the reality, however, is found in Christ."

Move Over

Apostle Paul challenged,
"Move over in your heart and make room."
That's what Jesus did when He emptied the tomb.
Not my will, Lord God, but Yours be done;
I'm willing to give so they can be won!

2 Corinthians 7:2 (AMPC)

*"Do open your hearts to us again
(enlarge them to take us in)."*

Unless

A rose is a rose is a rose

unless you know God who created it.

A day is a day is a day

unless you live it with God

who spoke it into existence.

A life is a life is a life

unless you allow the Giver of Life to indwell it.

Romans 8:11

"And if the Spirit of him who raised Jesus from the dead
is living in you, he who raised Christ from the dead will also
give life to your mortal bodies because of his Spirit who
lives in you."

Unfurl

Unfurl the ribbons of wisdom.
Unfurl the ribbons of revelation.
Cast them, cast them, cast them far.
How, Lord, how?
I am Your Aaron; I am Your life; I am Your fruition.
Unfurl Love's spools. Unfurl your gospel ribbons.
By prayer and meditation
send them out across the earth.
Trust, let go, and release everlasting mirth.
In My Word you've been wound tight,
and in the battle of faith
you've won the fight.
Your many ribbons are brightly colored.
They are of great value.
Unfurl, unfurl, and follow My call.

1 Corinthians 14:1

"Follow the way of love and eagerly desire gifts of the Spirit, especially prophecy."

Catch the Vision?

Is it like cupping your hands
to try to catch the unseen wind?
Yes, that would be true if that were all you could do.
You may not be able to see the wind
that turns a windmill,
yet round and round it goes.
You can't see your God who commissions you,
yet by faith His love unfolds.

The breath of the Almighty brings inspiration.
His vision for your life is beyond imagination.
Pray that Father God would instill
His manifested pleasure and divine will.

Ask for the desire that hope brings.
Receive your vision from the Creator of all things.
Look up to heaven. The sky is clear.
Take a deep breath. Listen and hear.
Throw back your head. Cup the hands of your heart.
Now catch His vision and be set apart.

Job 32:8

"But it is the spirit in a person, the breath of the
Almighty, that gives them understanding."

Job 33:4

"The Spirit of God has made me;
the breath of the Almighty gives me life."

Fullness

O Lord, how magnificent are Your ways!
The magnitude of Your vision
is forming — how large to me it seems
as I perceive Your dreams.
Your fullness has become my pavilion.
I have run in and found shelter
in the shadow of Your wings.

Ephesians 3:19

"... and to know this love that surpasses knowledge -
that you may be filled to the measure
of all the fullness of God."

Eternal Friends

Jesus, Lord, and Redeemer,
Who was and is and is to come,
You've called me no longer a servant but a friend.
It goes beyond understanding's height, width, or depth
when I ponder what it means to be called
a friend of the Author of Creation
and Finisher of my faith!
Infinity, that too is a word that shortens my breath.
I'm sure it's no surprise to You
that these truths seem out of my grasp.
But thanks be unto You,
God and eternal Heavenly Father,
that in and by Your creative majesty
You've found a way to impart a sense of knowing
that supersedes all that reasoning might say.
I am grateful indeed for Your eternal greatness
that lifts me beyond the limitations of mere humanity!
As the body of Christ, my friends are established as
eternal friends with You in the confession of faith that
declares You are Lord of our lives.

You have commissioned us to be of like mind and heart
with all our brothers and sisters in Christ;
to have friendships lasting forever — eternal friends.
People change, needs change, addresses change,
and yet Your love changes not! Because of this, I believe
that when friendships are born of You, they are born from
above; and like You, change not.
Best of all,
heaven-sent friendships continue through infinity
without reminders of the weaknesses in our character
that these beautiful friendships will continue throughout
infinity. What is born of God is born from above,
a gift and workmanship of Your grace,
making us one in Your abiding love.
We are and ever shall be friends in Christ eternally!

1 John 3:2

*"Dear friends, now we are children of God, and what we
will be has not yet been made known. But we know that
when Christ appears, we shall be like him, for we shall see
him as he is."*

Express

Tongues of expression form myriads of visions, flashing
on mankind's formations.
Express the invisible through the syllables
of the fadeless, brilliant Jesus.

Note the countenance of your Lord and fail not
to favor another so that same glory
may rest upon your face endlessly.
Fadeless, yes, the invisible becomes visible.

Compassion

The power of compassion will move through your eyes
and penetrate their soul,
piercing the depth of desperation they are experiencing in
their own search for love's denominator, Jesus.

Romans 4:17b

"...the God who gives life to the dead and calls into being
things that were not."

Matthew 28:19

"Therefore go and make disciples of all nations, baptizing
them in the name of the Father and of the Son and of the
Holy Spirit."

Mercy Leads

Mercy is the impetus to zeal.
Compassion the forerunner
of the purging, equipping,
fiery consummation of His justice.
Mercy is the catalyst that thrusts us forward,
fervently capturing the Kingdom of God
for ourselves and others.

James 3:17

*"But the wisdom that comes from heaven is
first of all pure; then peace-loving,
considerate, submissive,
full of mercy and good fruit, impartial and sincere."*

Found

I found happiness
I found peace of mind
I found the joy of living
Perfect love sublime
I found real contentment
When living in accord
I found joy for all time
Since I've found the Lord.
To the door of happiness
I found the missing key.
Jesus, lover of my soul,
You brought this harmony.

1 Timothy 6:6

"...godliness with contentment is great gain."

Balloons

Let's go, dear friends of mine.
Let's run with the new day.
We'll go see what we can find,
giggle, have fun, and play.
You blow up the balloons.
I'll tie them with strings.
Then we'll run as if we
had wind in our wings.
The clouds have been chased away.
God's mercy is new every morning.
His love is here to stay.
See the new day is dawning.
Let's wake the others still sleeping.
The day is ours for the keeping.

Psalm 59:16 (NKJV)

"But I will sing of Your power;
Yes, I will sing aloud of thy mercy in the morning:
for You have been my defense
and refuge in the day of trouble."

Gentleness

soft breezes

warm squeezes

simple instruction

careful production

The thought of gentleness feels like an embrace, and yet Father's Word says in Psalms 18:35 (KJV),

"*Thou hast also given me the shield of thy salvation: and thy right hand hath holden me up, and thy gentleness hath made me great.*"

Question:

Gentleness, my sought-out friend, issue from the throne, how is it you make one great?

Answer:

I never insist on my way with the unlearned and simple.

I lend to the poor and promote grace (Heb. 5:2).

I am born of good family.

I behave as a chivalrous knight,

giving another chance to choose rescue from plight.
I make a spacious place in understanding
to keep the feet from walking amiss (Psalms 18:36).
I quiet the soul as a weaned child.
Tender in manner and discipled by patience,
I nurture till strong (Psalms 131:2).

I, gentleness, astound the fearful by confident and
calm answers until to my side they are drawn.
The harsh become exasperated at my long-suffering
yet soon in frustration lament, turn to me, and cry out,
"How is it that you forbear?"
Fostering wise council,
I never insist on the letter of the law.
I am most fair and in my judgments quite equitable
for I am profoundly aware of Who created us all.

Response:
Gentleness has spoken tenderly to my heart
and prepared a highway within for my God
(Isaiah 40:1 & 3).
I can see the back of gentleness is strong and under

pressure will not quake. A smoldering wick it will not put out.

A bruised reed it will not break (Isa.42:3).

Gentleness' arms, one of mercy and one of compassion, have fed and gathered the lambs into my Lord's bosom. They guide those who are with young through the sheep gate of His promised wisdom (Isaiah 40:11).

Gentleness, I choose to know and trust you, ever surrendering to your ways. Just as you are God's child, so am I, and in like-manner shall lovingly spend my days.

Once I thought of you as only a kind favor,
but now I know your strength and ability to teach,
make great, and by liberty, deliver (Luke 4:18).
I applaud You, my Heavenly Father.
I am thankful for Your grace.
It is by Your workmanship of gentleness,
You are making me great.

Run with Grace

The greater the offense, the greater measure of compassion necessary. The insult is lost in the Insulted One — Jesus. The offense is lost in the Offended One — Jesus. That which grace began takes no pleasure in furthering by the legs of man. Robbery? It can seem so when grace's pleasure is not given full reign. Grace comes in full measure and desires to return the same.

But it has been said, "It is my appointment, my right, and my call. Shall I not be listened to by all?"

"Abomination!" grace shouts. "Would you leave me out? I, grace, who began a good work in you, will continue until I am through." Consider the promises, then consider your Lord.

Which shall you treasure; which shall be adored?

Shall it be said, "Thou fool, I require of thee this night." Or shall it be said, "War on, ambassador. Good fight!"

You are the chosen of God, a child of promise.

Come alongside and behold your Lord's face.

Consider the lilies, which do not toil or spin; and yet by striving, did you think you could win?

It's a race of redemptive forgiveness, a race that esteems the gospel mightier than personal presence.

So come hither, come higher. You will not be left alone. Don't be chagrined, but lift them up in prayer once again.

Set My Affection

God's love through the blood of Jesus procreates!
Life is both before and beyond heaven's gates.
Seek the difference between ownership and possession.
Embrace life in the Spirit.
Set your affection.
It is written, so listen and obey.
Eternal life is not quantity alone,
but quality life available each day."

No, world, you can't change my mind.
Life in the Spirit is a daily reminder
of His goodness, a memorial feast.
Yes, Lord, leaven the whole loaf,
from the greatest to the least.

You can't argue with love of this kind.
Yes, world, it's true. I'll never pledge my allegiance to you.
I've chosen the mount of blessing on which I'll stand.
His truth, His righteousness, gifts from my Savior's hand.
Jesus is the doorway through which I've entered in.
His sacrificial relationship has cleansed my sin.

My heart was once as the Passover's empty chair
until my Lord Jesus came and rested there.
Yes again, I've set my affection.
Jesus, You're everything to me.
Father, it's in Your holy election that I will live, move,
and have my being.
Your blood-bought prize I will remain.
Lord Jesus, lover of my soul, in me rule and reign!
Yes, I have set my affection
(2 Peter 1:7).

Thinking and journaling around the word *mystery* . . .

Romans 11:33 (AMPC)

"Oh, the depth of the riches and wisdom and knowledge of God! How unfathomable (inscrutable, unsearchable) are His judgments (His decisions)! And how untraceable (mysterious, undiscoverable) are His ways (His methods, His paths)!"

O God and Father, my heart swells with the thought,
You alone are infinite, with no beginning or end.
My journey to understand
is not of feet but only heart.
Let it begin!
In years to come, let its end be found far from its start!

Incomprehensible God, against all evidence
Abraham believed.
You are more than reverent reason can conceive.
Only Your revealed truth could ravish our hearts so,
and bring gratification to the intellect of seeking souls.

Your revelatory act of self-disclosure brought light to our
darkened minds, declaring who You are. By Your grace,
compel us to respond in transforming awe!
We can understand only the mystery
that You have freely given
and the rest remains aptly hidden
(I Corinthians 2:11, Colossians 1:27).

Once a man was caught up in paradise.
He heard inexpressible things. There is more to know
than he could tell! What a relief that truth brings.
I would be saddened and think less loftily, I'm sure,
if I thought we could express all that You are.

I am deeply grateful,
It strengthens my faith to know,
You are much more than just helpful.
Here I am a new creation, yet in many ways
still limited by Adam's fall.
Glory to God in the highest,
for He alone knows it all!

You are above, outside, and beyond all I can measure
or understand. Only babes of heart can begin to
comprehend the quality of life within each of your
children."
I know only what You've revealed.
I rejoice because You have attributes yet unveiled.
You, the cause of all things, yet caused by none,
with unsearchable riches and boundless love,
have brought my heart into a quieted place.
What a comfort to know You are beyond
even my inspired imaginings.

Your majesty extends
beyond what I could even hope to trace.
Surprise me. Overwhelm me.
Be mightier than I can bear.
Leave me breathlessly in awe
when I enter heaven's door
and see You there!

Laughter of Grace

The laughter of grace rocks my soul.
Grace's favor has lit the fire of perseverance.
Oh, patience, my welcome friend,
You've brought this trial to an end.

Diving into Love's Wonders

Secret wonders
Secret wells
An ocean depth of adventure
Discovering creation and its members
Diving deep
Declaring Scripture's thoughts about us
More numerous than the sands
Their vastness spreads into the expanse of eternity
Searching for Your love's wonders

Show them, Lord,
the wonders of Your love (Psalms 17:7).
Fulfill their many questions
with the magnitude of Your understanding.
As they immerse themselves in Your teeming life,
may the pressure of the depths not crush and confuse,
but instead release and infuse.
Grant freedom in Your realm so that they can see
it is done on earth as it is in heaven.

The innermost recesses of their hearts are crying out for
the depths of Your presence,

O God! Show them Your manifest glory.
I ache, yet I wait.
I pant, and I yearn.
My pulse beats out the command
to learn, learn, learn.
You set the earth on its foundations.
All creation responds to Your holy demand.
May Your glory be weighty upon their life,
causing them to dive
far below the surface of man's reasoning.
Make them divers in Your grace.
O God, how I want them to discover
the boundlessness of Your love.
Then, returning to the surface,
to escort others into the awareness
and magnitude of their discoveries.

Dear reader, what came to mind with these words was a picture of an ocean diver deep in water, enthralled with all that he saw. The Scriptures that follow came to my heart for you. I trust God hears the echo in your well, and all your desires are being met in Him. In the depth of His love, we celebrate this resurrection life!

Psalms 17:7

"Show the wonder of your great love."

Psalms 42:7

"Deep calls to deep."

Psalms 9:1

"I will praise you, O Lord, with all my heart,
I will tell of all your wonders."

Psalms 139:17, 18 (AMPC)

"How precious and weighty also are Your thoughts to
me, O God! How vast is the sum of them! If I could count
them, they would be more in number than the sand. When I
awoke, (could I count to the end)
I would still be with You."

Mystery

Jesus Christ, King of all creation,

was the humblest of men.

In what was termed "His triumphant entry,"

He rode a donkey into Jerusalem.

Then shortly thereafter

He died on a thief's cross,

accused of blasphemy.

Why?

To lay down His life for the sin of humanity.

Water to Wine

Jesus changed the water in Cana, at Galilee,
revealing His power to transform you and me
into His likeness, into His likeness.
Born of water, born of Spirit,
Water became wine,
His best is now mine.
Jesus changed the water in Cana, at Galilee,
revealing His miraculous ability.
Born of water, born of Spirit.
Into faith I was thrust.
In His workmanship I trust.
Only the servants saw the water change.
Only the one born again can see God's kingdom reign.
Jesus, my Lord, all has become new
since I've learned to draw from You.
God's love was transformed into the blood of Jesus.
By the gift of grace,
resurrection power has released us.

Born of the Spirit,
I've entered the blood-bought exchange.
Now bone of Your mercy and flesh of Your grace,
I shall remain.
The water and Spirit agree
wed with Your Word in favor and unity.
You saved the best till last,
love's excellence fulfilled.
What more could we ask as to Your mercy we yield?
Yes, Jesus revealed His glory in this gospel story.
He turned the water to wine,
declaring God's best would be mine (John 2).

Servanthood

Servanthood in Christ is a dignity and a delight.
It is the torch He carries,
the cloud by day, the fire by night.
While many in our day are saying
it's none of their affair,
our Lord Jesus desires that we reach out
and show that we care.
Don't inherit the winds of judgmental
or apathetic attitudes,
blowing dust in the face of need.
Let the mighty rushing wind of God's cleansing truth be
your passion and creed.

Leadership from a servant's heart
has less to say than it does to impart.
In heaven's hall of fame
is carved each servant's name.
Is it the price of entrance
Or only a kind recognition of significance?

The Master said that whatever you have done unto the
least of these, you've done unto me.
When we reach out to help others,
our Lord takes it quite personally.
God's not as interested in what always shows
as He is in what goes on when no one else knows.
Serving hearts have eyes to see and ears to hear
what the Spirit of Christ desires and holds dear.
It is time for your Lord Jesus' humble, loving ways
to captivate your heart and delight your days.

The word for *servant* in Greek, *diakonos*, consists of
two words. *Dia* means "through or across," as in the word
diameter, is a measurement through the center of a circle.
Konos may be translated as "dust, dirt, or earth." Thus
diakonos means "through the dust."

Mark 9:35

"If anyone wants to be first, he must be the very last, and the servant of all."

Diakonos in Mark 9:35 is the word used for the servant whose job it was to lead a family through a dust storm to find shelter, even if it claimed his life.

Your Hour

Prophesied: "Your hour, your hour!"
Think it not strange.
Now faith is, was, and ever shall be.
In moment, not memory. In fullness, not folly.
In patience, bringing forth fruit.
Faith is personal, collective, and corporate,
an enlistment, an enlightenment,
His direction, His manifestation,
His way, His truth.

A Tiny Crack

Will you look at that!
Unbelievable, isn't it?
How could that flower grow
In such a tiny crack?
Why, there isn't any room
Yet just look at it bloom.
I bet you nothing could impede
That stalwart little seed.
I guess it found a small shaft of light
And pushed its way.
What a sight!

2 Thessalonians 3:5

"May the Lord direct your hearts into God's love
and Christ's perseverance."

Hebrews 12:1

"Therefore, since we are surrounded by such a great
cloud of witnesses, let us throw off everything that hinders
and the sin that so easily entangles. And let us run with
perseverance the race marked out for us."

Temple

I am the temple of the Holy Spirit.
I house the brilliance of Christ within me!
Praise God, but how can that be?

"It's a gift, child, a gift from Me,
Your heavenly Father."

1 Corinthians 3:16

"Don't you know that you yourselves are God's temple
and that God's Spirit dwells in your midst?"

Cutting Edge

Mercy is the cutting edge of purity.
Triumph, the galloping horse of faith,
leaves judgment as the slain in the street.

James 1:27

"Pure and undefiled religion before God and the Father
this: to visit orphans and widows in their trouble, and to
keep oneself unspotted from the world."

James 3:17

"But the wisdom that is from above is first pure, then
peaceable, gentle, willing to yield, full of mercy and good
fruits, without partiality and without hypocrisy."

How Is Your Heart Doing?

A heart is priceless treasure hidden away. What authority
or standard decrees its value? Let me ask you, "Who is
doing this very important evaluating?"
We could watch it closely for a season to see from what
kind of soil it springs. After all, hearts have the capacity
to birth both good and wicked things.
What is it you are growing in your heart's fields?
How do you discern the quality and the bounty it yields?
If it is a gift from Him, Scripture says it will produce a
good harvest, thirty or sixty of a hundred times over.
Unlike some farmers,
you weren't commissioned to just grow clover.

John 7:24

*"Do not judge according to appearance,
but judge with righteous judgment."*

Mark 4:20

*"...like seed sown on good soil . . . produce a crop — some
thirty, some sixty, or even a hundred times what was sown."*

Talk to Father God

Talk to Me often, for I am near.
Talk to Me simply, for I do hear.
Talk to Me often, so I can be clear.
Talk to Me sincerely, so I can become dear.

New King

Once mighty flesh,
Abdicate the throne!
You shall no longer
Rule on your own.
Another has been
Crowned in your stead.
The authority is now removed
From off your head.

You thought you could stay the denunciation
Until a later time of consecration.
Aha, but in one swift thrust from the heart
Jesus Christ is crowned Lord and King
And you must depart!

Times of Love

Sometimes love roars,
Sometimes love laments.
Sometimes love is still,
Sometimes love is fervent.
Love faithfully endures
because God is omnipotent.
Love esteems others higher,
even when their desperate or
inconsiderate ways try her.
Love is quieted in peace by the
Author and Finisher of faith's increase.
Love is often asked to bravely surrender.
Her reward can always be found
in her God who daily commends her.
Love's desire gives to the helpless and wearing
thoughtful understanding and deeply caring.
Powerful, tender, and incredibly forgiving,
Love makes a way for a life worth living!

Hideaway in Grace

It was a bright morning and a full and busy day.
The colors had softened.
I could feel a gentle breeze blowing my way.
Closing my eyes, I took a deep breath
as I leaned back on the pillar for a rest.
Then to my delight,
I saw my dearest friend walking nearby.
She's like cinnamon on apples,
snuggled down in a warm, tasty pie.

She perched herself upon the gazebo wall
and together we watched the evening fall.
Her friendship is a spice well chosen, an accent flavor.
Her heart's intent is well spent, a sweet-smelling savor.
Even when our times are not bountiful,
she is a kindred friend.

When we get together again, she's graciously amiable.

Sisters in the Lord have a special place,

a hideaway in His grace.

Our times are a sumptuous dessert

baked to perfection.

When the evening ends,

I remain warmed by her affection.

Truth

Unlike the ups and downs of interest rates today,
Biblical truth will lead you only one way.
Possibly some would call you inflexible,
exclaiming your way is too narrow.
Truth is intolerant — its limits are not variable.
Narrow is the path that leads to life and
broad the way of destruction.
Within the bowels of truth
you find His life-giving instruction.

Today few think much about their spending.
"Until you're deep in debt, just buy on credit!"
It's an old familiar refrain.
When we follow its advice,
Oh. the pain, the pain!
The full revelation of truth shines in the New Testament.
Only by its light can we receive true enlightenment.
All that is symbolic or poetically understood
depends upon the literal for its parenthood.

We must not extend our doctrine
beyond Scriptural evidence
or spin just any hypothesis.
When interpreting biblical truth,
we don't have poetic license.
Literal may seem like such an enclosed word
with no room to breathe,
but it is a standard of safety,
a benchmark on which we may lean.

Rather than choosing what we believe
by what we like best,
we must study Scripture truth
within its proper context.
Truth's bank account is full and constant.
No matter how great or often the draw,
it remains abundant.
As we learn to spend only from what we find therein,
we never become bankrupt of truth again.

Hebrews 4:12

"For the word of God is alive and active. Sharper than any double-edged sword, it penetrates even to dividing soul and spirit, joints and marrow; it judges the thoughts and attitudes of the heart."

Inspiration

Alpha and Omega,
the scholars say that Your original manuscripts,
also called "autographs," cannot be found.
Yet written with the indelible ink
of Your inspiration, copies abound.
Author and Finisher of our faith,
we can see Your signature indeed.
Your name is written on every
page of the Holy Bible we read.

Everlasting Father,
we marvel as we study the unfolding evidence
of mankind's history and Your personal inscription,
revealing the glorious mystery.

Antiquity of the Ages,
branded on holy pages,
You left nothing to chance.
Your timing was just right.
You moved upon man
and caused him to write!

Voice of Many Waters,
wash us with the water of Your Word.
We submit to Your merciful sovereignty
and give You full dominion in our soul.
Cause ears to hear and eyes to see.

Almighty Creator of Heaven and Earth,
we stand in awe to acknowledge
that no mere coincidence
brought Your Word to birth
but instead God-breathed providence!

Spring

The most meaningful springtime you will ever know
is the one that blooms in the hothouse surrounded by snow.
Its yield knows not the exterior's cold lament.
Instead, it profusely abounds in a sweet-smelling scent.
(Jesus was and is the earthly precedent.)
The measure of its beauty shall never wither or fade.
It remains safe from temperature's
every whim and cannonade.

The hothouse stands, as someone once coined the phrase,
"in the dead of winter."
And yet within the length of its days
we can see plants and flowers grow,
displaying their splendor.
Yes, it's a fair and wonderful thing,
this hothouse filled with spring.

The Lord's Supper

There was a host of people gathered 'round,
making a clanging, grating kind of sound.
Supposedly they were there for communion,
but it appeared to be no more than noisy confusion.
Then a sober lament from on high was heard:
I have no praise for you.
Your meetings do more harm than good.
You come together, and among you are divisions.
Some have brought abundance
while neighbors are left without provisions.
Some are getting drunk
while others remain hungry.
Have you no respect for Me
and My blood-bought family?
You despise My presence and humiliate others.
Is this the love Jesus taught
you as sisters and brothers?
No, indeed not.
He is not pleased with these ungodly actions.
I admonish you—

Esteem others as higher than you and your desires.
Dispense with your self-serving factions.
Share with one another in love
instead of gluttony and strife.
Celebrate the cup of the New Covenant in His blood
and the precious gift of new life.
The Lord's Supper was meant to be observed
in right order and manner from a sincere heart.
Therefore, do not participate amiss,
but examine yourself before you take part.
This is a holy communion to be shared
with a common benefit
in reverent submission to God and sweet fellowship.

Jesus said, "In remembrance of me,
. . . take, eat and drink worthily."
Be cleansed of your sin.
Abide in Him.
Proclaim the Lord's death and resurrection
until He comes again.

Touring with Him

Holy Ghost,
take the Church on a tour of the death and resurrection
of Christ Jesus once again.
Amaze our hearts with a revelation of Your provision.
Surely then we will rejoice with joy unspeakable.
Sweet Savor of Life,
permeate us. Our joy will be a hint of heaven to everyone
we meet.
Great power comes from the stillness of trusting faith.
From the joy of Christ strength is procured.

Perseverance

Often when perseverance finds a way
And then looks back upon its path,
It discovers — lo and behold —
It was not chance when it took its stance,
But the way was appointed from of old.

Buttercups Under Ice

How foolish, some would say,
you're always hoping tomorrow
for what didn't happen today.
Always? Yes.
Foolish? I don't think so.
After all, why not believe it will happen on the morrow?
Only fear holds back trusting once more.
Consider the peaceful spirit hope has in store.
Let go the fear you won't be able to bear the pain
if you find your hopes were embraced in vain.

We must remember life extends beyond this hour
and to trust God's loving care
and willingness to empower.
For those who have eyes to see,
even nature preaches a hopeful tale.
And what is her good news?
There's reason for hope beyond each dark veil.
Consider creation and the many lessons we can learn
from the flower, butterfly, or silkworm.

You've seen the photographs. I have too.
Remarkable, what a wonder, wow!
What seemed impossible was true!

One marvel through a photographer's lens
in the Teton Mountains
was buttercups blooming under ice —
a captured phenomenon of life.
If the picture had not immortalized it,
who would have believed it could be so?

Few would know
that buttercups could grow
not only in the severest cold
but bloom from beneath ice surrounded by snow.

Nevertheless, there they were.
My heart leapt in affirmation.
It's true, God's mercies are sure.
I stood there, awed in admiration.
Hope, like a winter bridegroom,
expectantly lifts the veil of obscurity,

revealing that God's commitment to you
goes beyond the moment into eternity.
Most assuredly there are seasons in our life
when we need to remember buttercups under ice.

When you're overwhelmed,
and tears rush down your face,
don't forget the buttercups
emerging from beneath the icy lace.
Scripture warns that hope deferred
makes the heart sick.
Heaven's voice within can encourage
when hope seems thin.
Buttercups are blooming
where you cannot see.
They are nature's reminder
that earnest expectations, concealed,
at any given moment may be revealed.

If your blossoms don't come into full view,

lean on Father God to strengthen you.

Until the last night is done and the last breath taken,

my hope will endure long, resting in God's salvation.

How about you?

Do you believe His Word is true?

The English of My Heart

God of the jot and tittle,
the punctuation of my heart,
You are the Comment and the Comma
and the Exclamation of my soul.

You capitalize all Truth
and period all evil.
Your questions of conviction bring
statements of correction.
Your Son Jesus is the Completer,
my Connector
to Eternal Life!

Sweet Grace

Taste and see. The Lord is good.
His strength is made perfect in weakness.
The nectar of Jesus
is His grace to accomplish.
Satisfaction, fulfillment, obedience —
where can these be found?
In the sweetness of His grace
God's power abounds.
Psalm 36:7-9

Made in the USA
San Bernardino, CA
31 January 2019